Cardinals

D1289960

by Stan Tekiela

Adventure Publications, Inc.
Cambridge, MN

Dedication

To Paul Dahlgren, a thoughtful man of wisdom. Thanks for being part of my life for so long.

Acknowledgments

Thanks to the Bird Collection, Bell Museum of Natural History, University of Minnesota (St. Paul) and the All Seasons Wild Bird Stores in Minnesota, which have been instrumental in obtaining the seed images in this book.

Thanks also to Jim and Carol Zipp, good friends and bird store owners, for reviewing this book.

Credits

Cover photos of birds by Stan Tekiela

All photos by Stan Tekiela except pg. 25 (top inset)

Edited by Sandy Livoti

Cover and book design by Jonathan Norberg

10 9 8 7 6 5 4 3 2 1

Copyright 2015 by Stan Tekiela
Published by Adventure Publications, Inc.
820 Cleveland Street South
Cambridge, MN 55008
1-800-678-7006
www.adventurepublications.net
All rights reserved
Printed in China
ISBN: 978-1-59193-528-5

Table of Contents

All About Cardinals

For many, the Northern Cardinal is the most favorite backyard bird. The brilliant red plumage of the male, the bright red bill and black mask of the female, the strong and clear mating song announcing the arrival of spring, and the devotion to family make this a highly desirable bird to visit our feeders.

Cardinals exhibit strong sexual dimorphism, with males appearing much different from females. The flashy feathers of the male advertise his health and virility, while the dull colors of the female help camouflage her while she incubates on the nest.

The Northern Cardinal (*Cardinalis cardinalis*) is a perching bird, or passerine, in the Passeriformes order of birds. This huge order includes all perching birds and also birds that sing. Cardinals are a rare combination of good looks and amazing sounds, with a well-developed voice box (syrinx) that enables them to sing. They are also one of the few bird species in which both the male and female sing beautiful songs and duets, oftentimes on warm, clear days with blue skies.

Mates form strong monogamous bonds and stay with each other all year. During spring and summer they work together to defend a territory. When winter rolls around they become gregarious and gather with many other cardinals as well as chickadees, nuthatches and goldfinches in mixed flocks.

Facts

Relative Size: the Northern Cardinal is slightly smaller than an American Robin

Length: 8–9" (20–23 cm)

Wingspan: 10–12" (25–30 cm)

Weight: 1.6 oz. (45 g)

Male: bright red with a distinct black mask, large red bill, pointed red crest on head that the bird raises and lowers at will, gray-tinged tips of feathers during winter

Female: dull gray with red flecks, black mask, large red bill, red tip of crest

Juvenile: same as female, gray-to-black bill, short crest

Nest: cup; 4–5" (10–13 cm) in diameter, 2.5–3.5" (6–9 cm) high; female builds with a variety of materials from the surrounding area

Migration: non-migrator

Food: seeds, insects, fresh or dried fruit, comes to seed feeders; favors black oil sunflower seeds, also likes striped sunflower seeds, safflower and cardinal mixes

Range & Habitat

The Northern Cardinal has adapted well to urban and suburban environments. Originally a southern bird, the population increased dramatically over the past 150 years and has steadily moved northward into Canada. Cardinals now inhabit the entire eastern half of the United States and parts of the Southwest. In Canada they have settled into Ontario, Quebec, New Brunswick and Nova Scotia.

The expansion of bird feeding in the past 100 years enabled these birds to reach new habitats where they were never before seen. Cardinals are now thriving in a wide variety of habitats, from forests to prairies and deserts to subtropical regions and more. They are making their homes in forest edges, thick native shrubs, cultivated shrubs and small trees around homes, as well as in scrublands and deserts, utilizing desert shrubs with sharp, stout thorns for safe cover.

● Breeding Season

Songs & Calls

Our Northern Cardinals are favored for their wonderful songs. Unlike many North American songbirds, both the male and female sing. Except during nesting time, males sing more than the females, and pairs sing in magnificent duets around their territory.

In January and February, adult cardinals sing subsongs. These are practice songs for the breeding season and the first ones that young cardinals learn. Adults sing in earnest during March and April to establish territories and attract mates. Males with more song types attract more females. You may hear them singing well into August, when some pairs are still continuing to mate.

To maintain contact, males and females give short, non-musical, metallic-sounding chip notes singly or in a series. They indicate alarm, territorial aggression, food squabbles and much more. The frequency and volume of these calls increase with the level of agitation.

QUICK-TIPS

- Cardinal songs sound like "whata-cheer-cheer-cheer," "birdy-birdy-birdy" or "what-what-what"
- Songs have 5–12 syllables, last 2–3 seconds and are repeated after a pause of 5–10 seconds
- Each individual has 10–12 unique song types, but some very expressive cardinals can sing more than 25
- Cardinals in northern regions sing a slight variation (regional dialect) of the songs sung in southern states
- Cardinals identify the locations of others with slow chips

Nests

Northern Cardinals are reported to nest in more than 50 species of trees and shrubs. Pairs visit several potential nest sites before starting construction. Sites tend to be in protected, concealed places such as forest edges, prominent shrubs, clumps of vegetation and fencerows. The female chooses the spot, and the pair sings a duet before building begins. The male may bring in small bits of material, but mainly he watches for predators and also interloping males that might try to breed with his mate while she builds.

Cardinals usually build 4–8 feet above the ground, but nests can be upwards of 40 feet high in trees. Young females make flimsy nests, while experienced females build well-constructed nests that will withstand storms. No need to put out materials for them. Females select weedy plant stems, grapevine tendrils, strips of grape-vine bark and other plant material, and line the interior with fine grasses, rootlets and dried leaves. The interior portion of the nest is very important because it provides a microclimate for the eggs and developing chicks.

During construction the female often sits on the nest material to shape it. She leans back and forth to imprint her body and tamps the bottom with her feet. Most construction occurs early in the morning, but building goes on at any time of day during the second and third broods. Usually it takes 3–6 days to complete a nest, depending on the weather and availability of material.

Eggs, Chicks & Juveniles

Northern Cardinals can raise up to three broods per season. In the warmer southern states, they have more broods with fewer eggs per season than in the cooler northern states, where there is less time to produce additional broods. Thus, cardinals lay eggs at different times regionally. At birth, chicks are naked and helpless and cannot regulate their own body temperature. The mother must continue to sit on them (brood) until they have enough feathers to keep warm. The male brings in the most food for the chicks and the brooding female.

Within just 9–10 days of hatching, the chicks leave the nest (fledge). By this time they are juveniles, nearly full size and look like the female except for their dark bills and smaller crests. They follow their parents around and beg with beaks open, fluttering their wings and squawking. Adults land nearby and feed them.

Broods: 1–3 per season

Clutch Size: 2–5 eggs (3–4 average)

Egg Length: .9–1.1" (2.3–2.8 cm)

Egg Color: grayish blue or greenish white and heavily marked with brown or purple

Incubation: 12–13 days; female incubates the most

Hatchlings: naked except for sparse tufts of down feathers, with eyes and ears sealed shut

Fledging: 9–10 days

Cardinal Trivia

- The cardinal is the official state bird of seven states.

- Named for the red robes of Roman Catholic cardinals.

- Called "Northern" to distinguish it from other cardinal species outside of North America.

- It has a thick beak, but it's not a finch or grosbeak. Cardinals are members of the Cardinalidae family.

- Most live about 5–6 years. The oldest cardinal on record lived much longer—15 years and 9 months!

- Cardinals obtain their red coloration from carotenoid pigments in the food they consume. The more they eat, the brighter red the feathers.

- The bright red plumage causes Cooper's and Sharp-shinned Hawks to target males over the dull females.

- Occasionally cardinals replace, or molt, all of their head feathers at the same time. This leaves the birds bald, exposing their black skin beneath.

- Cardinals sunbathe! They fan their tail feathers, spread their wings and lay across a branch or on the ground. Often they raise the feathers on their heads and backs and open their bills wide. These sunbathers enjoy the sun's heat for several minutes.

- Mainly ground feeders, cardinals eat mostly seeds and readily visit feeders. They love black oil sunflower seeds and also like insects and fresh and dried fruit.

- Human table scraps are unsuitable food for cardinals.

- Male cardinals defend territories of about 2–3 acres during the breeding season.

- Cardinals are not territorial during winter and gather in small flocks of up to 20 individuals.

- It is thought that large highway bridges over wide rivers provided resting spots for cardinals in flight and helped them expand their range.

- Because cardinals usually feed on the ground, some people think that snow depth may have limited their expansion northward.

- Cardinals are known to attack their reflections in windows, car mirrors, hubcaps, bumpers or other shiny surfaces. They do this throughout the year but mainly during the breeding season. Seeing its own reflection, a cardinal attempts to drive the "intruder" out of its territory. It can spend many hours attacking the reflection with its feet and beak, often damaging its feathers and leaving marks on the object. When the level of aggressive hormones diminishes later in the season, the attacks decrease.

- The male cardinal strengthens the pair bond with his mate by feeding her during courtship (allofeeding). The female postures like a juvenile bird and accepts his food offering.

- A courting male will occasionally sing a song and perform a flight display. He fluffs his feathers, raises his crest and flies to the female with his head held high and flapping with short, rapid wing beats.

- City parks provide good places for cardinals to nest.

- Most cardinal nests have a high degree of vegetation protecting them from at least two sides.

- By the time female cardinals start building their nests, they are already fertile and ready to lay eggs.

- Sometimes a female cardinal will start building a nest, only to stop and start someplace else. Other times she will build an entire nest, lay her eggs and then move on to another site. The reasons for these odd behaviors are known only to the bird.

- The male finishes feeding the young of one brood after the female leaves to build another nest for an additional brood.

- Well-concealed nests have the same rate of plundering (predation) as nests located out in the open. Also, the height of the nests from the ground has no effect on predation rates. Perhaps this is why cardinals nest in a wide variety of places—there is no single factor that promotes their safety.

- Studies show that cardinal nest success rates increase in suburban areas as opposed to rural and wilderness areas. This may be the single reason why cardinals are expanding their range.

Feeding Cardinals

Attracting Northern Cardinals to your yard is easy. When there is food, water and shelter, they will come. Cardinals feast on seeds, large numbers of insects and their fair share of fruit, depending on the season. They eat mainly seeds in winter and switch to mostly insects in spring and summer. During late summer they feed on fresh fruit from shrubs, vines and trees, including dogwood, sumac, mulberry, hackberry, raspberry, wild grape, tuliptree and buckthorn. In fall and early winter they enjoy the dried fruit left from the summer months.

Cardinals have large bodies and small feet, so feeders with large landing surfaces are best. Providing a variety of feeder types gives them many choices of food for a balanced diet. See pages 35–37 to learn more about the types of feeders to use for cardinals.

Water sources can range from a simple birdbath to a complex waterfall. A shallow depth of 1–1½ inches works well since cardinals need to stand to bathe or drink without being submerged.

Shrubs, vines and trees near feeders, and man-made structures, such as fences and arbors, provide safe living essentials and shelter. While shrubs and trees serve as staging areas where cardinals can check for danger before flying to feeders and birdbaths, garden structures offer cardinals places to nest.

Seeds, Grains & Legumes

Black Oil Sunflower: Studies have shown that Northern Cardinals prefer black oil sunflower seeds over all other commercial bird foods. Black oilers are smooth black seeds that come from the common sunflower plant, *Helianthus annuus*. Cardinals have no trouble cracking open these seeds with their large, strong bills.

Black oilers contain more fat in the form of oil than other seeds, hence the name. They are meatier and pack more nourishment per bite than just about any other bird food on the market. Each seed has a nutritional value of 28% fat, 15% protein and 25% fiber, and supplies vitamins B and E as well as calcium, iron and potassium.

Striped Sunflower: Striped sunflower seeds have a thin white stripe. They are larger than black oilers, and they have a thicker hull, making them harder to split. Nevertheless, cardinals open them easily and like them immensely. Occasionally called stripers, these are the sunflower seeds that people eat. High in fat, protein, vitamins and fiber, they are usually a part of any popular birdseed mix.

White Safflower: This is another good food for cardinals. Smaller than black oil seed, safflower is a thick-shelled, small white seed that is high in nutrition and fat. The shells lack a definitive seam and are hard to crack, but cardinals use their thick, heavy bills to open them without problem. These seeds come from the annual safflower plant, *Carthamus tinctorius.*

Golden Safflower: Enjoyed by cardinals, this is a hybrid of white safflower that is also called NutraSaff safflower. Introduced in 2004, it is a specialty seed with high oil content, high protein and polyunsaturated omega–6 fatty acid. Developed as food for beef and dairy cattle, poultry, fish and bird feed markets.

Hulled Sunflower: Hulled sunflower is just the meat or nutmeat of the sunflower seed without the hard, inedible outer shell. The nutritional content is the same as black oil and striped sunflower seeds. There is no possibility for these seeds to germinate, so the bags are marketed as non-germinating or no-mess mixes. With hulled sunflower, you won't need to rake up or blow away discarded hulls under your feeders.

Hulled sunflower is often available as whole nuts or pieces or chips. The expense of shelling the seeds makes this feed more expensive than others, but the benefits may outweigh the cost. After all, most birdseed is sold by weight, and with hulled sunflower you are not paying for the inedible shells.

Milo or Sorghum: Milo, also known as sorghum, is a very good food to offer cardinals in western states. They enjoy this seed, so offer it in a tray ground feeder or scatter some directly on the ground. Solid blocks of seeds contain mostly milo. These last a long time and feed many birds.

White Millet: Millet is a soft-shelled, small round grain that comes from the millet plant, *Panicum milieaceum*. There are red, golden and striped varieties of millet, but the most common for bird feeding is proso millet, which is white.

White millet is not the most favorite seed of cardinals, but it contains good nutritional content: 4% fat, 12% protein, 8% fiber, vitamin B and calcium. An affordable seed that is usually offered in ground and tray feeders, it is also sprinkled on the ground to attract cardinals to the feeders.

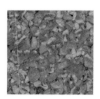

Cracked Corn: At a wonderful low cost, cracked corn is a great option to feed large numbers of cardinals on the ground. It also attracts rabbits, squirrels, raccoons, opossums, and other birds. Offerings of cracked corn will keep the squirrels busy with something to eat, leaving your feeders filled with the higher priced foods for the cardinals alone.

Cracked corn is exactly what it sounds like—dried whole corn kernels that have been cracked. There can be a lot of dust associated with cracked corn, but it's worth it. This food won't sprout and grow in your garden or lawn, and cardinals eat the entire kernels, so there's no waste. Low in fat but high in protein and fiber, it is often a base in bird food blends. Offer it in large open-tray, fly-through or ground feeders or sprinkle it around the ground.

Whole Corn: Whole corn consists of entire kernels of dried corn and is often part of the base of wild bird food mixes. It is less desirable to cardinals than cracked corn and usually is thought of as wildlife food since it attracts squirrels, chipmunks, raccoons, opossums and other animals. You can offer it in a large tray or trough ground feeder or spread it on the ground.

Peanuts: Peanuts are another option to feed cardinals. The peanut plant, *Arachis hypogaea*, is a member of the legume or bean family and grows underground. Peanuts contain 45% fat and 24% protein, and they are a good source of vitamins A and E as well as zinc, iron and potassium.

Peanut pieces are popular in seed mixes and suet. Cardinals will eat them in any form—shelled, in small chips or whole in the shell. They gobble up peanuts quickly, so sprinkle them with a feed mix or place them in a feeder with a tight mesh to prevent large amounts from spilling out all at once.

 You can also try offering peanuts in the shell to cardinals. Put them them in a larger mesh feeder with large openings so the birds can extract the entire nut. Peanuts get wet and tend to mold, so avoid putting out a lot at one time.

Mixes

 **Cardinal Mix:** Just about every major retailer has its own version of a cardinal mix. It is almost always a combination of black oil sunflower seeds, striped sunflower seeds, safflower, cracked corn and other ingredients. The amount and proportion of seeds vary from store to store, but the main seed in these mixes are black oil seeds. To start getting Northern Cardinals to come to your yard, offer a cardinal mix.

 Premium or Deluxe Blend: Premium blends are often a base of black oil sunflower seeds combined with striped sunflower seeds and safflower. The addition of peanuts, shelled or whole, upgrades any regular blend to premium or deluxe. Sometimes these mixtures also contain raisins, cranberries or other dried fruit. Cardinals love this rich food, and it is great for winter when you want to offer an extra special treat.

Non-germinating Mix: Non-germinating mixes are composed of seeds that have been removed from their shells. Because seeds without shells will not germinate, people who don't want rogue sunflowers growing in their lawns or gardens may want to try it.

These mixes often have 2–3 varieties of seeds, with whole nuts or pieces of seed meat. Non-germinating may look like the most expensive seed per pound, but you're not paying for hulls, which are included in the weight of other seeds but aren't eaten.

Specialty Mix: Many seed stores make a specialty blend that is unique to their store and works well for their region. In eastern states, black oil sunflower seed is the main ingredient. Western states often offer mixes with a heavy portion of milo. Stores may also mix more peanuts or cracked or whole corn with seeds.

Other Foods

Suet: Another way to attract cardinals is to offer suet. Suet cakes are composed mainly of beef fat. Specifically, it is cow fat from around the kidneys and loins. However, more and more suet is coming from cow fat anywhere on the animal.

Suet is an extremely high-energy food with a high calorie count, and cardinals easily digest it. Some varieties are mixed with seeds, nuts or dried fruit. Suet in these forms is a great way to give your cardinals an especially tasty treat.

Offer suet in specialized wire feeders with a bottom perch. These allow cardinals to reach into the cake and break off small pieces. Hang the feeders from a pole or fasten them to a post. Protect suet feeders from squirrels, chipmunks, raccoons and opossums, which will take the entire cake.

Mealworms: Mealworms are the worm-like larvae of darkling beetles, which are flightless insects. An excellent source of protein, calcium and vitamins, the offering of mealworms will attract cardinals as well as a variety of birds that don't normally come to traditional seed feeders.

Mealworms can be purchased live or dried. Both are sold in large quantities, and for good reason. When cardinals find them, they gorge themselves. Live mealworms must be stored in a container from which they cannot escape. A steep container with slippery sides is essential, and it should be refrigerated. Offer dried mealworms in a shallow tray.

Fresh & Dried Fruit: Offering fresh fruit, such as orange halves, is a popular way to bring in cardinals. Many fresh fruits, including bananas, apples, melons and grapes, and dried fruits, such as raisins, currants and prunes, are good choices to put out.

Cardinals will come to orange halves placed sunny-side up and impaled with a nail to secure them. Fresh fruit slices can become messy and attract insects and mammals. To keep animals away, provide the fruit on a platform with a squirrel or raccoon baffle.

Grape Jelly: Cardinals also like the sweet taste of grape jelly. Cardinals come to this highly sugared, high-energy food early in spring when the weather can be cold and wet. Many types of commercial jelly feeders are available, but you can offer the treat in a small tray, cup or other device. To prevent the birds from getting jelly on their feathers, offer small portions each time.

Peanut Butter: Regular smooth or chunky peanut butter is another good food to attract cardinals to your yard. Offer it like suet in specialized feeders or just smear it on a chunk of bark, directly on a tree or on a suet cake. You can offer this high-energy food in your own creative ways. However you present it, cardinals will quickly find it.

Storing Birdseed

Storing birdseed safely is easy. Keep it out of the house, preferably in a cool, dry place away from direct sunlight. Garages and sheds are the best places to stow feed since the cooler temperatures there will reduce the number of grain moths hatching out of seeds.

Transfer seed out of its original plastic or paper bag into a clean container. The container should be upright, semi-airtight and prevent mice, chipmunks and other rodents from chewing through and getting to the seed. Metal garbage cans are good choices for storage. Use several to store different kinds of food.

Try to avoid buying bird food in very large quantities. Pick up just enough to feed cardinals for a month or so. Make sure you use up the oldest seed before opening your more recent purchases.

Feeding Q&A

Black oil and striped sunflower seeds— what's the difference?

Black oil sunflower seeds have around 70 percent nutmeat compared with just 57 percent in striped seeds. They also provide more calories than striped seeds in the form of fatty oils.

Should I stop feeding during the summer?

Summer is one of the best times of the year to see and feed cardinals. An appealing array of food offerings draws more cardinals to your yard and makes bird watching at home even more active and exciting.

What if I leave town or take a vacation?

It's not true that when you start feeding cardinals, you can't stop. Cardinals do not become dependent on our feeders. They take advantage of the quick and easy offerings, but once those are gone they just fly off to another feeder or a wild food source. When you get back home, simply fill your feeders and watch the cardinals return. It won't take long.

What should I do with old seeds?

Birdseed can go bad over time. If seeds smell bad, the oils have gone rancid and the batch needs to be thrown out. Grain moths, spiders and other pests can infest old birdseed. While bugs won't affect the overall seed, they may be trouble in the house. Wet seeds will spoil and stick together. The resulting mold or mildew can be fatal to cardinals, so discard seeds at the first sign of decay. Sprouted seeds are also red flags for disposal. Rodent infestation means urine or feces in the seed and you should not use it.

I have a birdbath. What about mosquitoes?

Birdbaths are essential for most backyard feeding stations, but mosquito proliferation is a concern. There are products that release a larvicide, killing all mosquito larvae, but a much more natural solution is to prevent them from developing at all. Moving the water with a small waterfall or battery-powered water wiggler does this, or simply change the water. It takes about seven days for mosquito larvae to develop, so use your garden hose or a bucket once a week to keep them in check.

Water, even in winter?

Cardinals always need water to drink, so a shallow offering anytime of the year is good. Heated birdbaths will attract many cardinals in winter. If your birdbath is deep, add less water or a layer of small rocks to make it shallow. Water shouldn't be more than an inch or so deep because drenched feathers will freeze quickly in extremely cold temperatures and ground the birds.

Bird Feeders

Offering assorted foods are sure to attract Northern Cardinals and keep them coming back. A good feeder for them has a large, flat platform and lots of headroom. Called fly-through platform or tray feeders, some styles also have a roof.

Larger hopper feeders with large places to land and feed are also good choices. They don't need refilling as often as tray feeders, which hold just thin layers of seed.

Cardinals readily come to tube feeders with perching pegs for easy feeding. Some have multiple tubes.

To attract cardinals to the millet or cracked corn in your ground feeder, scatter the food around the area nearby.

Cardinals love to feast on mealworms, either live or dried, especially during nesting season. Be sure your container does not allow live mealworms to crawl out.

QUICK-TIPS

- The most versatile types of feeders and favorites of cardinals are platform, hopper and tube feeders
- Choose platform feeders with a roof to help keep snow and rain from covering and soaking the seeds
- Hoppers hold many seeds and also keep them dry
- Tube feeders with a base for spilled or extra seeds give cardinals a place to perch while feeding
- Ground feeding maximizes your chances of attracting cardinals to your feeding station

Feeder Types

Platform, Tray or Ground Feeder: Also known as a fly-through feeder. Usually has a flat, open surface for seeds. Hangs from a series of wires or chains, rests on a central post or pole, or sits on the ground with the bottom of the tray about 12 inches off the ground. Made of wood or metal and often has a series of holes or slots for water drainage. Some have a protective roof.

Hopper Feeder: Often made of wood or recycled material. A central storage area, called the hopper, holds a large number of seeds, which are slowly released. Seeds are visible through the plexiglass sides, so you know when to refill.

Tube Feeder: A clear plastic tube with feeding pegs at metal openings for accessing seeds. Small to large sizes hold different amounts of seeds. Some have a bottom tray for extra seeds, which cardinals use as a landing platform. Hang from shepherd's hooks or set on top of posts or poles.

Window Feeder: Made of lightweight plastic or wood. Suction cups adhere these feeders to window surfaces, allowing for close viewing. Many types of foods, such as seeds, mixes, mealworms and fruit, can be used in window feeders. Be sure to check the Food & Feeder Quick-Chart on pages 40–41 for some of the best combinations to offer cardinals food.

 **Suet Feeder:** A treated metal cage that holds a preformed cake of suet. Cardinals feed easily from styles with a stand at the bottom for perching. Some have a roof, which sheds rainwater and accumulations of snow and protects the food from bird droppings. Hangs from a chain or attaches to a post.

 **Mealworm Feeder:** Usually plastic with tall sides. Material needs to be slippery so live mealworms can't crawl out. Many kinds of dishes and trays exist to feed cardinals this treat. You can also recycle a plastic food container and fashion your own design.

 **Mesh Feeder:** Constructed with metal mesh to hold peanuts. Usually consists of a long tube large enough to hold a plentiful supply of nuts. Small openings for peanut pieces, larger openings for peanuts in shells, and cardinals need to work at getting any out. Releases only one peanut at a time.

Placing Feeders

Feeding cardinals is our pleasure, so always put feeders where you can easily watch and enjoy them. They should be near an area in your home where you spend a lot of time and in a comfortable place where you can see outside clearly.

Most feeding stations are about 20–40 feet away from residences. Placing feeders closer draws cardinals to where you can easily see them. However, the closer the feeders, the more likely you will have window strikes.

Feeders close to shrubs or other cover give cardinals a place to stage and look for predators before flying in to feed. Plant cover also gives them a quick place to hide in case a hawk swoops in. Feeders in the middle of large open spaces usually don't attract many cardinals.

Place feeders where squirrels can't get to them. The basic placement rule is 5 feet and 8 feet—meaning feeders should be at least 5 feet off the ground and at least 8 feet from any other surface from which a squirrel can jump. This includes trees, houses, sheds, charcoal grills, birdbaths, patio furniture and anything else a squirrel can climb to jump onto feeders.

When placing feeders, be sure to install a squirrel or raccoon baffle on each one. Baffles are metal tubes that prevent these animals from climbing your shepherd's hooks and accessing the bird food.

Remember to do some ground feeding. This style of feeding attracts many cardinals, so you'll want to scatter seed around your yard, but not in your flower garden. The constant scratching by the birds and the mat of hulls and shells that accumulates will kill any plants you are trying to grow.

Choose a place with where seed waste won't kill the grass. Perhaps landscape an area of the yard dedicated to bird feeding with rocks, shrubs and a water element.

Multiple feeders bring in larger numbers of cardinals. Cardinals perching on each of the feeding pegs prevent more individuals from accessing the seeds, so place more feeders to accommodate the other birds.

Provide a variety of feeders to attract more cardinals. If possible, choose one of each type to offer a nutritious, well-balanced assortment of food.

Food & Feeder Quick-Chart

Northern Cardinals enjoy a variety of foods at different times of the year, and they also eat from a variety of feeders. This chart lists the foods in the preferred order for the assorted feeders.

FOOD	Platform, Tray or Ground	Hopper	Tube	Window	Suet	Mealworm	Mesh
Black Oil Sunflower	●	●	●	◐	✕	✕	✕
Cardinal Mix	●	●	●	◐	✕	✕	✕
Premium or Deluxe Blend	●	●	●	◐	✕	✕	✕
Specialty Mix	●	●	●	◐	✕	✕	✕
Striped Sunflower	●	●	●	◐	✕	✕	✕
White Safflower	●	●	●	◐	✕	✕	✕
Golden Safflower	●	●	●	◐	✕	✕	✕
Hulled Sunflower	◐	●	●	◐	✕	✕	✕
Mealworms	●	✕	✕	◐	✕	●	✕
Grape Jelly	●	✕	✕	◐	✕	✕	✕
Peanuts	✕	✕	✕	✕	✕	✕	●
Suet	✕	✕	✕	✕	●	✕	✕
Fresh & Dried Fruit	◐	◐	◐	◐	✕	✕	✕
Milo or Sorghum	◐	◐	◐	○	✕	✕	✕
Non-germinating Mix	◐	○	○	◐	✕	✕	✕
White Millet	◐	○	●	○	✕	✕	✕
Cracked Corn	◐	✕	✕	✕	✕	✕	✕
Whole Corn	◐	✕	✕	✕	✕	✕	✕
Peanut Butter	✕	✕	✕	✕	○	✕	✕

FEEDER TYPE

● Best   ◐ Good   ○ Acceptable

Maintaining Feeders & Good Practices

Feeder maintenance is essential for the overall health of Northern Cardinals. How often you clean your feeders depends on the weather and season. Cleaning is more important during summer than winter, and feeders in wet environments require more cleaning than those in dry climates. Bird feeders offering food with a high fat content, such as suet, need to be cleaned more often than those holding less fatty foods.

Bird feeders are the number one place where disease is spread among bird species. Dirty or contaminated feeders hold bacteria, mold and viruses that can sicken or kill the birds.

A number of transmissible diseases are associated with birds, including cardinals, and their droppings. To be safe, use good hygiene practices and take some basic precautions when filling or cleaning your feeders.

For example, when you clean the feeders, wear rubber gloves. After filling or cleaning feeders, vigorously wash your gloved hands and cleaning brushes with warm, soapy water. Use paper towels to pat dry, and discard the towels.

Cleaning Your Feeders

Always try to use rubber gloves when handling your feeders and cleaning the feeding area because there are several diseases that can be picked up from bird droppings. *Histoplasma capsulatum* is a fungus in soils that is deposited from bird and bat droppings. It is recommended to wear a particulate mask while raking up or blowing away seed hulls underneath feeders. Many people who contract histoplasmosis don't develop symptoms, but some exhibit mild flu-like symptoms. Rarely, other people can suffer serious complications.

Cryptococcosis is another fungal disease found in the environment, and it also comes from bird droppings. Often associated with pigeon droppings, it is best to wear rubber gloves and a mask when cleaning up scat on feeders and around roosting sites, attics, cupolas and other places where large numbers of birds gather. Like histoplasmosis, many people don't suffer any symptoms. Some just come down with symptoms of a mild flu.

West Nile virus is carried by mosquitoes. Cardinals and other birds contract it but don't transfer it to humans, so there is no need to be concerned about getting this disease from your feeders.

Keeping your feeding station clean and refreshing the site are quick and easy ways to stop the spread of avian disease and other diseases from bird droppings.

A quick dry-clean is recommended each time you refill your feeders. Dump out the old seeds before adding any new and knock out any seed clumps. Also, wipe down the feeder with a dry rag to remove the bird scat before refilling it.

You should wet-clean your feeder if there are obvious signs of mold or mildew. Dead birds near feeders or on them are another indicator that a major wet cleaning is needed. Use a sanitizing solution of one part bleach to nine parts warm water, or purchase a commercial bird feeder cleaning solution.

To remove stuck birdseed, use a scrub brush. Insert a long-handled bottlebrush in tubes, and use an old toothbrush to clean other hard places to reach.

Dismantle the feeder as much as possible and scour with your scrub brushes and cleaning solution. Clean inside and out and rinse well with hot water. Allow the feeder to dry thoroughly overnight or lay the parts out in the sunlight before reassembling and refilling it.

Cleaning around the base of a feeding station is very important. Rake up or blow away old seed hulls on the ground. These will accumulate after a long winter or other extended feeding. Add or refresh any mulch or gravel beneath your feeders.

Finally, remember to wash and rinse birdbaths before refilling them with fresh water.

Protecting Cardinals

The U.S. Fish and Wildlife Service estimates there are 10 billion resident and migratory birds breeding in North America annually. By the end of the nesting season, there are about 20 billion birds.

The majority of threats to birds are associated with people. Collisions with building windows are one of the biggest killers. Nearly 100 million birds die each year from flying into windows. During migration through cities, they fly into lit skyscrapers at night. Most small songbirds migrate at night and seem to navigate better in darkness than with artificial light. Businesses in tall buildings are starting to douse their lights during migration, and this has helped.

Collisions with windows also occur at residences. The reflection of sky and trees in windows and glass doors creates the illusion that the flight path is clear. This causes tragic window strikes at home. To see cardinals close-up and protect them, move your feeders to within 3–5 feet of window and door glass. This prevents the birds from gaining too much speed on takeoff and reduces impact. Move feeders to least 30 feet away from windows to stop collisions due to reflection.

You can also apply ultraviolet (UV) light reflective stickers to glass so cardinals can see objects instead of reflections. These stickers are clear and often have the shape of a bird. While we can see through them, the outside reflects UV light, which cardinals can see.

Studies show the most effective way to reduce window strikes is to hang ¼-inch-thick metallic streamers from the eaves of your house in front of windows. These streamers block the path of cardinals in flight. There are many more ways to reduce window strikes, so be sure to check online for more solutions.

Before the bird feeding industry was established, it was common to put table scraps outside for the birds to eat. Very few people would waste any food, so often it was just stale bread or tidbits of other old food. However, cardinals don't accept morsels of this type, and this kind of feeding usually draws critters, such as skunks and raccoons, that are not welcome in backyards. So whether you set out attractive ground feeders or simply place food for cardinals on cut tree stumps, it is not recommended to use table leftovers for bird feed.

According to one study, pesticides are responsible for killing an estimated 72 million birds annually. Most of the pesticide use is agricultural, but you can support the efforts to reduce the chemical ingestion fatalities of birds in several ways.

It's easy to help by purchasing only fruit and vegetables in season. Buying only organic fruit and vegetables is another option. Taking a step further, you may decide to go organic in your own garden and backyard. Reducing or eliminating your personal use of pesticides and her-bicides will not only make the overall environment safer, but the cardinals you love will eat uncontaminated fruit and insects as they stage near the feeders in your yard.

About the Author

Naturalist, wildlife photographer and writer Stan Tekiela is the originator of the popular nature appreciation book series that includes loons, eagles, bluebirds, owls, hummingbirds, woodpeckers, wolves, bears and deer. For about three decades, Stan has authored more than 120 field guides and wildlife audio CDs for nearly every state in the nation, presenting many species of birds, mammals, reptiles and amphibians, trees, wildflowers and cacti. Holding a Bachelor of Science degree in Natural History from the University of Minnesota and as an active professional naturalist for more than 25 years, Stan studies and photographs wildlife throughout the United States and has received various national and regional awards for his books and photographs. Also a well-known columnist and radio personality, his syndicated column appears in more than 25 newspapers and his wildlife programs are broadcast on a number of Midwest radio stations. Stan can be followed on Facebook and Twitter. He can be contacted via his web page at www.naturesmart.com.